A Morsel of

a Quarter of Time

A Morsel of

a Quarter of Time

poems by

Grace Rodriguez

ISBN: 978-0-578-67764-4

This book is my redemption and
each poem is dedicated to you,
who's been gifted another chance to
give the bull's eye a blow.

Contents

Preface

Poetry feels so intimate; every line seems to creep inside me, sort of repaints me blue within. No need for images or objects to act as a medium; everything is conveyed to emanate emotions that purge me out of reality, like I'm in an alternate universe I, myself created. Writing is the only way I've ever felt human, like my life is full of possibilities and I have forged the key to a door of ambivalent opportunities. Time, on the other hand, is a complex but beautiful thing; sometimes it can feel like an eternity, and other times it feels overwhelming, like we can't get a hold of it because it is seeping away in our fingertips.

Time does not coincide with our modus operandi because it works in its own favor, but it is generous; it gives us a lapse of chances daily, like an all-you-can-eat buffet on the clock, although we're constantly wasting its offerings and blatantly blaming its chart.

This book is the physical representation of time and I dovetailing at last and giving birth to this phenomenal catastrophe.

I say this because the term "now" was hard to grasp for me; I would always dodge it, stalling around it with the excuse of starting tomorrow or "what is meant to be will eventually happen," when in truth, I was my own hindrance. It was up to me to start the engine.

I've always had a vision, and that is to contribute to history, make my own part in it so even after I'm gone, my name can live on. I want to inspire others and create something worth existing. I want my books to be my legacy.

So, with that being said, let me simplify it for you: writing this book was probably the best thing I've done in my life thus far. Although it didn't happen as smoothly as you would think. I didn't have it all figured out up until today, as I'm writing this. I had no clue how I wanted it to look like; I just knew I wanted people to read it.

A Morsel of a Quarter of Time is a huge chunk of me pasted on paper, and in a way, I don't know how I feel about it other than… exposed. It's like I've invited people inside my subconscious, and now they will see how the creative process looks like.

Just as I refuse to share my playlist with anyone, I don't condone displaying how my brain functions. I've never liked the idea of putting myself out there because that's like standing in the middle of a big crowd at a concert and expecting to look different from everyone else around you. Knowing I'm not as unique as I like to think scares me, and that fear is a weakness I would much rather stray from.

It took blood, sweat, but mostly tears, to give this book a heart to beat, throb, and breathe on its own. And although it is far from perfect, it's unapologetically honest and true.

Before you step on my threshold and raid my mind—surely invading my privacy— hear me out.

A Morsel of a Quarter of Time is a poetry collection shedding light on the transience of being and finding oneself; an anthology exploring self-esteem, feigned sanity, and the many lively struggles of solitary adolescence. It reflects the internal darkness of a worn-out soul with the guts to push through the arduous, leaden days that seemed to have no end. All by myself: a scrawny, pallid girl with no social skills and an abysmal self-hatred. It is far from perfect, but if I were to look in the mirror next to it, I would see the resemblance; the fact that we're equally imperfect but somehow good enough.

So, here is a chunk of me to you—my first attempt, raw and real, unfiltered, with its flaws, holes, and oddities.

Now, this belongs to you. I hope my words become your company, I pray they speak to you and make you feel a little less tainted.

Outsider

Twisted stomach, jaded eyes.
Let's talk about what makes my insides
burst,
what makes me want to puke—
the fiery-lipped truth splitting off the wood,
riven by trivialities that scrape my wound
for your absolution.

Cheers to my favorite grudge—
the one I personally enjoy most:
your cherry-flavored insults,
the semi-dangerous, rather exciting stuff.
Sigils from the afterlife scribbled across my
spine—
the root of all demise.

I learned to give you everything I have
and watch as you demolish it
with your sketched hand and polished
tooth.
I do not like the feeling of being an
outsider,
of watching through the sidelines
when the spotlight was made for me,
but I hold back—

I always hold back,
because you are trapped in my bowels.

There's no point in trying to compete with
you
when you are always in control,
when you are the stem of thorns
strained through my nostrils.

Satiny, translucent petals
of a classic red rose—
the one everyone's destined to love.

Malevolent Entail

My tongue is a razor blade
that cuts crumbs of you,
tastes pieces of silkworm
and mistakes them for your blood.

I am the art form of heartache;
some say I am the chills
of deflection and deviation.

I feed off disillusionment
and emit a whirlwind of notional hope.

I move around like a fretful snake
with a sly grin,
loiter within your anomalous instincts
and make them go motionless.

An algorithm with a clear target—
a feculent plan,
searching for a way to expand,
dip inside your nerves,
sleep under your skin.

Planting pencil pines on your back
and calling them designs,
making you moan when I inflict pain.

A malevolent entail of your secret reality—
the bridge between repose and vitality.

Blubber Knives

Seraphim—chaste, tidy, holy—
You claim to be so adequate;
it makes my viscera shriek and wallow,
my head twist, and you proceed
to swizzle it all with the condensed thrust of
rum.
Pour the vodka as the calypso strikes up,
raise it to the ceiling, and pull down the
curtains
when your mom arrives home.

I purge your lies, vent your libel,
and toss it away, but you double-cross me.
It feels like catharsis—
nothing but mere repressions
and senseless confessions,
as if another carnal man
could ever save you.

You know what you have become,
what you've always been deep inside.
You feel no remorse, no regret
for what you hide.

You pretend too much, thinking
everyone looks at the profile you put on
display,
but I'm not like them;
I deploy, unfurl, and debunk it.

I don't taste your drink,
so you can't poison me mid-sip.
Angels don't hide their tails
inside their pants;
they don't carry blubber knives
around to point at the smaller fish.
You'd stifle your own friends
if it meant you'd have the whole ocean to
yourself.

Fear

Look at the sky as the golden hour arises—
How the moon arrives in what she knows as
perfect timing.
It winces at the sudden change,
drastic blackout; now the darkness takes
over once again.
Wilted clouds hibernate—
a stint of inactivity for a lapse of time.

Tell me, were you scared of what you could
no longer see?
I wonder: what if everything we know as
"good" would turn "bad" at the fall of
night?
Diseased with the same sickness of the
wicked,
the major reduction in bone density—
Who would save you now?
What would give you certainty that not
everything could go wrong?

The truth is, we're constantly taking risks,
even the loosest of us all.
Choosing to trust makes us feebly human
every time.
We all feel fear, ample or small.

Don't think that makes you special;
we all struggle with that—
an unpleasant feeling triggered by our own
perceptions of life.

A half-empty glass could drown you in
your own lies;
sweet dreams of discord.
Oh, don't you wish you could disconnect
from this side of the vehicle?
It speeds up at the sight of a stop sign;
you're bound to crash.
Set into thinking how an erudite passenger
like you ran with that luck—
Would you astray from your material
condition if you still had the chance?

Life and Death

There's something about walking on the
edge of existence that trips me out.
Today, we are here; tomorrow, who knows?
A doubleheader balcony, a train pulled by
two locomotives coupled together—
Once you fall on the other side, you can't
get back up; it's time to rest.
Life nurses us far too much,
no matter what it brings to our cradle, we
always want more—
We want to witness what death can give at
the inlet of misery, defy the womb that
nurtured us.
Life and death: sisters at birth and mortal
enemies at once,
born from the same limb but bound to bear
inverse incomes—
different offerings written with the same
quill.
Life lives in fear, praying death doesn't
break the accord,
snatch them off her breast before they can
fly on their own,
before they've even grown wings to flutter
around.

Life and death fight a lot,
their armies trained to do the same.
Death—acrid and sullen, barren and
cursed—eager to steal life's offspring to
have someone by her side.
Death steals from life to feel satisfied,
to feel equal and competent,
even if life's creation will soon disappear
and cease to exist.

Proxy Divine

Find shards of me underneath your entrails;
my mangled youth relies on your fingers.
Grotesque images of your smile
surf in my mind all year round.

I've gone mad before—
I know what it feels like to be petrified
by the annihilation of my own brigade.
The carcass of my soul stacks up yellow
grenades,
neatly arranged in case there's another
massacre,
in case I fall in love again with the idea
of someone who's not ideal—
someone who looks like you:

Silky lips and captivating eyes,
alluding to small pillow talk and scented
candles,
in the fragrance of lively nights.
Proxy divine; silver lining spilling over
the echo of your furtive pleasure.

My head rests on your chest, and in this
moment, I can breathe—
I've been set free.
You're all I need when I've lost sense of
who I am.

But I know it's wrong, I know I shouldn't
have gotten attached
to a whit of heed.

Love is not what I aspire to be.
Love won't pay my bills or feed me daily.
I can't catch up to you because
I'm just a chore in your calendar,
a nice sample of whatever you're feeling
that day,
and I will never stick around for more than
a hot minute.

I guess I can say I've learned from the best,
so, I won't allow my heart to catch feelings
again.
I hope one day we meet face to face,
when you're fresh and untouched,
to sweep you off your feet—
one day when the apprentice supersedes the
master dean.

Expectations

Enigmatic, formidable, and sage self-
esteem,
looking back at me from the ledge, whilst
dissociating from my reliability.
The future holds a treasure up its sleeve,
with my name engraved on it,
but you tell me it's a mistake.
You make me feel like I'm not worthy of it,
like it belongs to someone else instead.

Living life, gritting my teeth through
banquets of expectations;
when pessimism fails to scupper me, it
reins me in.
Survival comes with horrid drafts—
the general consensus might disagree,
but damnation does not always roll in
through mislay.

Sometimes it's the result of our perception
of victory that leads us to perdition.
Sometimes we want what we shouldn't
have.

But who dares tell us we can't delight in the
sun?
Even if it incinerates us,
we'd still picture the plain of wildflowers
spread like patchwork under its embers.

Ever Present

Gutter of memories—
Shutters close, and streams of blood
outspread like orchards in the river,
like planted aloes, or cedars amid the
waters, distilling from our vile hands.
Shredded verses that were spared from
poetry—
Maybe I hide behind metaphors of what
once was,
somewhere only those who decode my
figure of speech will find me.
I am ever present, with different faces—
never permitted to be considered anyone
less than me.
A whisper of time, an arcane notation.
I am half asleep,
amid being awake and being deliberate,
but I am also hapless, regal—
surely embroiled with cobalt tension,
cooled and molten mixtures of flush.
I am lying on a cushion stuffed with
spires—and you are the first thought that
breaches my mind.

If my words were fragments of fume, I
would strip them of their grey shifts and
garb them in tint,
but maybe that's just me.
Maybe typhoons are the result of grounds
wailing to be plunged, marine limbs
longing to be touched.
Maybe I am more than you ever deserved—
a foreseen masterpiece bigger than your
ego.

Navel-gazing

"Bull crap" is the terminology of
something that's incorrect
because it doesn't coincide with your way
of thinking.
So, it's not correct, simply because you
don't agree.

I learned this from your rebukes and
interjections when I spoke.
Nothing I ever said was quite precise to
you,
which led me to think frivolity must be
short for your name.

A tiny cadre of qualities you contain,
an outburst of everything untamed within
you—
the animation of the rotten apple you harbor
inside.

You tumble, roll, and skid down your
rambunctious hatch of lies;
your tongue is your defecation.
You focus so much on your own wit,
you don't recognize how much you don't
know.

Nature despises you because you believe
the world is yours.
You turn to your grueling navel-gazing,
vigorous demeanor; no mirror needed to see
it's all about you.

Patterns

My hoarse voice can intone melodies,
metrical songs off-key,
but you'd still remember me.
Like contusions and scars, I'm drawn on
your skin, marking territory.
Venom glands contract to push the poison
out the fangs; I serve my purpose.
Asserting authority with my parasitic lyrics
and enticing web,
catching all listeners who wander through
my realm.

I chose to bleed like this,
so I might as well live up to it.
A rathe blow to the battered crowd;
retort, matey sound from the heavens
above.
Some call it talent, I recognize it as a
granted gift—
to play around with words, use them to my
advantage—
or at least that's what you thought.

But really, I just enjoy talking a lot,
(to myself, because talking to others has
never been my expertise).

I spit them heavy,
put a mask on the spot for people to acquit
their creativity,
break old patterns,
and build new ones out of tragedies.

Anger

Oh, human scheme,
pulling out the worst in me;
brisk brain and spry soul—
The decadence of your coalition scintillates,
seething emotions fighting to persevere.
Taking the flint and steel from your satchel,
casting sparks upon the torches,
erupting into complete conflagration.
A glimmer of rifled thoughts splutters,
fast, frictionless, swirling,
constantly sending mixed signals.
Alighting the flame like emulsified
kerosene—
taking hold of me,
endeavoring to add susceptibility to
everything.
The sediment settles quickly,
matter that regulates my instincts,
leaving me palsied,
prone to serious thought.
I feel this anger skirmish under my skin,
pressure building until I can no longer
breathe.
My spattering mouth begins to spill words
I am not accountable for.

Nostalgia

I've been trying to find my way—
somewhere in my memory, my hands were
made of almojábanas,
just like the ones my grandma used to make
for me.
A scalpel represents incision, but I'm not
ready to let go yet.
Some say it's time to do the cutting.

At night, when I can't sleep, I stare at the
ceiling
and watch as it changes locations—
from plain white to wooden brown.
That's when you realize:
the smears of old paint in the corners make
a huge difference.

Topsy-turvy days, the bed seems
backwards;
linen shroud—
a winding sheet of hope that things will go
back to normal.

But I know time has worn out,
and nostalgia is a phony falsifier.

It keeps making me feel like back then
things were better,
but my life wasn't as nice as I remember.

Though it hurts to be so distant,
like an uncharted region of space,
I don't get to see my loved one's face.
But it is always a thrill to know I found
myself.

Canary Yellow

When you kissed me, time thickened like
tension,
wanting to stop, but it wasn't up to it.
So, seconds continued to seep through my
skin,
readily becoming hatched minutes—
contracting my ailment.

Like globs of paint on the cupboard of my
soul, you stained me;
and I swore I shone in canary yellow,
bulldozing the city surrounding me,
like an ordinary bee thinking she was the
queen of the hive.

Lemon gunk hoping to be a sweet, sweet
orange,
tired of scrubbing dirt off the floor.
Sometimes it's nice to feel less like a
speckled egg
and more like a sugarplum.

Sometimes I just want the world to taste me
and not spit me out like insipid gum.

Departure

Every morrow is a munificent band
that binds us to this universe we live in.
The despondency of what we've lost
bribes what we wish to strive.
No alms of any kind can restore
what we've worked so hard to accomplish,
because shekels nor gold can buy effort and
sweat.
We are wreathed in vast success,
from waking up each morning to resting
every night.
Our knees turn to chalk as we crawl
towards the doorstep—
and sometimes it's hard to leave
what our hearts recognize as home.
Weariness drizzles our eyelids, and we
struggle to stay woke,
but when it's time to go,
we must go.

Immortals

Even immortals have weaknesses;
we're all bound to abscond death's wing,
scuttle our way out of its lugubrious
prison—
an unknown paradox floating
somewhere in a distant dimension,
shepherded nowhere in particular.

Daggers, white oak, and ravaging fire;
wastelands of fainting, gusting, throbbing
hunger.
The desire for blood, the need for flesh
and snapping veins—lashing out,
tearing villages to the ground
to feel whole.

But our fear of love is what we all have in
common;
our consequential, never-ending, lingering
debility—
like wolfsbane and vervain,
love weakens us until there's nothing left,
no more than a void in our chests
that overrules us until we retaliate,
turn to ashes or children of disaster.

Perhaps that is our fate:
going against nature's way,
cursed by its fury and consuming rage.
We're all bound to break—
nothing in this life is infinite.

A Morsel of a Quarter of Time

Don't mind me when I say
I'd stop time for you,
because I will most certainly try to.
The universe depletes my favor,
but not in my defense.
I'll hold onto you solemnly;
halt this instant,
stretch it from one side of the horizon to the
other.

In a morsel of a quarter of time,
I'd ransom your eyes from losing all sight.
I'd tell the sky your secrets
and watch it dismantle at my touch.
I'd make the ocean besiege
at my proposal to let me
make a home out of it just for the two of us.
I'd water your field with the galaxy's tears,
yet you'd still ask me why.

In the end,
I would be so eager to wake up next to you
that I'd end up slipping away,
averting from your gaze
like a translucent hurricane.

Solitary Years

I met her when I saw her in her truest, most
vulnerable state—
the side of her she hid behind layers of
paste and thick mascara.
When her coconut-scented hair was in a
bun and the sun couldn't quite touch her.
Where no one else could see her but me,
I felt her pent warmth—
the one she called weakness and refused to
show.

I saw her draped in her own guilt and
apprehension,
groping for her stranded possibilities.
I wonder when she collapsed so direly;
from good to volatile so quickly,
solitary years in the making.

The curtains remain mid-open,
enough room for the wind to sneak in,
but closed enough for hope not to barge in.
The door chimes, and rueful thoughts stroll
in,
pilfering any mite of motivation lingering.

She drank a gallon of sedatives,
hoping to subdue her impulses.
I find bits of glass scattered across the hall,
from broken promises—
remnants of permanence she stepped on and
forgot to clean.

Caving In

The door is bent.
Oh, I've done it again.
I've pushed everyone away, and I'm not
ashamed—
I'm caving in.

Inside this reckoning, restoration is
undertaken.
I am arranging a flower bouquet with
weeping dicentras,
placing it on the table, hoping someone will
spray them—
brimming with hope so that they can be
reborn.

I am chanting words to dilute with
wormwood—
vermouth and absinthe,
aromatically sealing the cottage so that no
one intrudes.

It is all about perception—
the protective barrier to ward off the aliens.
I differ—
opposites fathom why agreements disband
when there is a mutual pledge.

The fabric has been dismantled,
and the roads have gone their separate
ways.
This chapter has concluded,
but the story persists—
unfolding despite the threat of defeat,
inexpressively thrilled to see the summary.

Hazardous Line

I take two steps back to reassure my
posture—
perhaps I've been walking too avidly,
mutinously,
like a toppled soldier.
I have hidden too much of me
and televised only what seemed perfect.

Steadfast loyalty to a veracious image—
I walk a hazardous line;
I've deserted my feelings,
and I can no longer reach them.

I now am what I anointed myself to be—
this automaton created to be distinguished,
in hopes of writing history,
(the modest kind).

Lower the portcullis,
pull up the drawbridge;
my fears and I
have welded together into one frugal lie.

Telegram

I love how your skimming fingers make me
feel
when you press them tightly into my skin;
how I can't get enough of you
even after all these years.

You float around my mind like a copper
fly,
make it your chamber,
and decorate its columns in a flaming red.
You are the prospect of my hair turning
gray
when I reach fifty-one,
the silent colloquium that is my mind.

I like to point out that you are
the prettiest diminished piece of art
I've ever laid eyes on,
and my most intricate desire,
denoting purity tucked away
in a corner of my soul;
the opaque telegram that traces my body,
leaving my insecurities out of the picture.

Two-fold Façade

Most of the time, I presume to understand
life,
understand why it picks us up like flowers
from a den
and places us in front of a hassle.

I look at my surroundings and always hope
for a better outcome, wish upon a blissful
end-note—
maybe even a brief intermission.

I bathe myself in my own conviction
that one day life will leave us to rest,
or give us a happy momentum to hold onto
before death comes to lug us away.

I do this every now and then.

I'm just beginning to realize
that life has a two-fold façade,
and once you understand how much decree
your state of mind has over it,
the weight of the world becomes more
brittle.

I Don't Belong

Rifting time in half—dented into the
cosmos,
asteroids, planets—space that does not
abide by me.
I don't belong;
I'm wafting around a billow of air
that doesn't blow for me.

I'm buried alive;
mandarins palliate my havoc
when I'm not an abuzz volcano making
new land—
aboard on my hand.

Let me tug you in,
allay your calvary when life has goaded
you.
Allow me to salvage what's been ousted
and skewed out of the bulwarks.

I am reined in,
leaning over the parapet when the pavement
is right beside me.
I think it is safe to say
I'm better off skipping or crawling;
either one would do better than walking.

Sand Dunes

I marvel at memories, surmounted by
muffled voices—
buried six feet under when the longest
strands are stunted.
Surrounded by sand dunes,
suddenly, everyone wants to build a castle.
I shudder, not in terror,
but in exhilaration—flanked by a built-in
trance.
I outmaneuver consular players,
brooding over the need to find a tactical
gambit.
Roosters begin the serenade of crow,
atop the mound formed by rapid winds.
Grit in my eye; the tempest unfolds,
and I snicker with amusement, for there are
no wonders to behold.

Mourning

I let it slip—my consciousness,
and turbulence ushers the tenebrous void,
awakening a poignancy that is bound to
impinge on me—
The starlet of a cataclysmic reverie,
where you still prowl my contemplation,
and I fail to abstain.

You're somewhere deep inside a forest
where there are no verdant trees,
no sunlight or cool breeze.
If regret could take it all back,
I would bewail my words until I can no
longer speak,
until there's nothing else to be said.

I would buy you this world if it meant
I'd keep you in it.

Hunger for Pride

When the dust settles,
she is the fine residue of ashes,
lodged into the monolith—
the legacy of neglect, lulled to sleep.
She holds this world with her mere hands,
dispelling all dejection,
but no one is there to thank her for it.

It's all part of the narrative:
the repetitive cycle of dereliction and
betrayal.
Everyone is familiar with time,
but no one knows effort.

She is by herself,
aware of the odds of breathing in the
smoke.
After the frenzied attack,
they wait until the panic's out—
an insatiable hunger for pride.

Arrival of the Stork

We crawled underneath the scorch marks
from the fire that saw us originate,
and the old skeletons were set aside
to accommodate new remains.
The walls recite secrets only the deaf will
retain,
hiding little tragedies as the bell rings.
Copying onto slate, hewing timber,
as the arrival of the stork retires from our
presence.
This is the essential banality of our horror
stories;
we will only deteriorate.
If we are lucky, this might be a swift
recovery.
Beware; an act of valor can always lead to
rebirth.

Acanthus Motifs

While you explode on a whim,
I'm weaving tapestries—
old pictures painted in glory;
acanthus motifs and countless ornaments
to foment peace.

I gifted you a handkerchief
with my monogram on the corner,
but the washing machine must've
swallowed it.

A lavish, unpalatable feast
of radical assonance and alliteration,
generic abstractions of what love truly is,
trapped inside brackets
because parentheses are too wide.

A luxurious collection of equations
no one dares to decipher,
but alas, I try.
You demonstrate once again
that my absence is the only thing
you've come to appreciate.

My Name in Past Tense

You call that girl my name in past tense,
pronounce her dormant instead of dead,
as if she governs my concordance,
and has a latent hunger for tactical
replacement.
She is simply a compendium of what's no
longer innocent—
barbed memories of probation.
Her smile seems evanescent.

The fabric of her dress does not fray,
unsightly garments of a futile yesterday.
Her birthdays sound more like pity parties,
reverberations of a futuristic diary,
rumbling and delirious, scorned with
derision.
Her eyes are the torrid heat of a summery
morning.

She is not an old version of me;
I can't claim her if she's someone else's
creation,
when she still bleeds.

Fervid Cigarette

You are possessed by deceit;
your pretty brown eyes look down on me
from the never-ending precipice.
You make me feel as though I am all you
can see,
but that is never a good thing—
for you howl at me, spit at me,
make me savor the raw insults
you've clearly thought about in the comfort
of your room.

You shun my beliefs,
wrap my hair around your fist,
and feed me my buried insecurities—
for I have no teeth to chew,
no tongue to speak,
and no voice to scream at the seared
cicatrix on my chin.
Your fervid cigarette is now part of me.

Brink of Doubt

What leads to confidence, to certainty?
There has never been resolution in your
sublime words—
continuously cutting through the fatigue,
always sounding more like snippets of
chagrin,
proclivities for mishap—
leaving me bereaved and stranded.

With your lofty avarice,
dithering about a narrow gorge with no way
out—
A brink of doubt.
Your tenets of coarse speech and
belligerent demeanor
feed on my impotence.

Let's start over—
there is no creative avoidance.
My nimble fingers can't type accurately;
I'll recite instead—
an even limber tongue will do the trick.

What questions must I answer?
Which reflections stare back at you
when the call goes mute?

If I am falling, so are you.
I want to be in the bottomless pit,
laughing at your mediocre falsity.

No longer will I degrade myself for your
sake;
so, mask the grief as you lead to despair.

Amber Fantasy

She is a vibrant rarity—an amber fantasy,
florid orbs that outstrip gold.
She is the daughter of night and day—
the link between luster and nobility,
and the auburn surrounding the iris.

In gloom, she is nocturnal chestnut,
brunette complexion—
a pure stroke of serendipity still.
I'm convinced she's some type of miracle,
coppery hue with flecks of melanin.

Russet and citrine—
a vibrant trait of mystery and harmony.

Rising Phoenix

Who taught you to dream like this, bleed
like this?
You are the most resilient thing I've ever
seen, girl.
Priapic, piquant little bird—
snapping and rattling,
always taking the long way home.

Peculiar, diminutive thing,
you get your wings in a twist, and they tell
you:
"From dust to dust, young fowl,"
but what they don't know is
you were made from incense and myrrh—
you are a resurrecting, crescent thing,
a rising phoenix in a mason jar.

You will not be pulverized,
neither dead nor alive,
so, pick up the pace;
you are an œuvre d'art,
still throbbing, still growing,
constantly evolving.

One day you will detach from this shaft;
you will become your own mantra,
no doubt in my mind,
a stellar rumble gravitating towards the
light.

Head or Tales

"Let's play a game," he says.
"Head or tails?"
He then flips the coin,
sounding as inviting as ever—
nothing wrong with betting the odds.

A meager girl,
she opens her puckish maw
and swallows nothing but her own tinted
fluids,
the acidic cerise bubbling like foam.
She's oblivious, as far as I'm concerned,
so invested in his starlings—
kestrels and robins—
granted by the enchantress;
he licks this plot of land dry.

He baptized himself in wild frenzy,
wears his crown of ivy,
and drinks his cup of wine.
A kaleidoscope of colors stains her
conscience
as he delivers the astral climax of his
speech;
he must always make her flinch.

"What is it that you want?" she asks.
But he is a Greek god in pursuit
of something bigger than the ecstasy of
being alive;
his theory of attraction subverts the rule of
law.

Periodic Man

Saying sorry is exalting you,
giving praise for taking the hit
when you unleash your whip.
You, a pompous arachnid
with the cruelest pincers.

A periodic man cloaked in rot,
used to drinking his coffee black and raw,
as obscure and crude as the morning news,
and you are the spokesperson.

I want to say I'll survive this one,
but the truth is, I don't know.
When you hear a paused silence followed
by a sudden *boom*,
do not hold your breath, and do not expect
the worst.

It's always in my best interest to hang
around the floor,
tilt my dizzy head against the almanac
so he knows I'm listening.
My qualms, assembled at his behest,
penetrate my psyche.

His knuckles are a dynastic parable,
an oeuvre in stylus.
When they caress my cheek,
they imprint a carnation flower,
and I smile with my front teeth,
bite off its petals and leaves.

I never knew love could be depicted like
this,
so migrant and resonant,
like a whirlwind of energy constantly
charging.
I am the current, and he the receptacle;
I'm eternally flattered and grateful
because he depends on me.

So, tell me,
is that really such a bad thing?

Vendetta

Slumped and disheveled,
our multi-chromed manor clashes in.
A vendetta drawn against us,
betrothed to our heads, sodden in dread
and blustering revenge.

Logic says it is survival of the fittest,
so, it's you or me—
You're a sinner, and I'm a sin.
Today you are dovelike,
tomorrow an artillery, ready to blow up
this whole sphere.

I hear you loud and clear,
the sound of your voice cutting through the
social strata
like bankruptcy. Sometimes it's simple,
like a sheet without wrinkles in the
cracking blaze
of the ornamental hearth,
welding parchment to the stone.

Archival and missionary,
a passage dashed with entrées
to commemorate the debt underlined
and italicized by the reverend.

In your self-aggrandizing code of conduct,
you prevaricate when responsibility breaks
in.
It is time to confess,
atone for your piacular impulses.
Blessed or dismissed, it all comes down to
this.

Mystified

My doltish feelings get in the way
oftentimes;
my cognizance is a malady
that has mystified the observers.
Like burs clinging to my wool socks,
it hurts when I walk—
I can't bring myself to talk about what's
bothering me.

Neglecting what is not worth mending,
as if primitive failure were nonexistent.
Fables that simulate betrayal
when the bulk relies on one side of the table
because that's how it shall always be.

A lenient penalty,
mordant sense of enlightenment
where dissociation occurs.
My perception, de facto divided,
relegated to a secondary role,
as if this world could care any less
about my evocative dilemma
of nourishing the intellect or assuming
tolerance.

Silhouette

I am a figment of your imagination,
a contorted photograph folded into the
creases of perception;
a spade to my essence,
to sculpt a generalized image.

Breathing in the sycamore trees,
the tinge of genteel maroon in the tarry
breeze.
I release you—liberate you from my
underwing.
You're on your own now,
with enough room to float on the shawl of
your impost,
but lesser hands to ignite the fire.

Luciferin leaks through your abdomen;
I'm lactose intolerant to your shapeshift.
Milky way into dulcet torment,
veering midway from an overdose.
A fatalistic result;
I don't know how to get out of this rabbit
hole.

The unimportance detonates,
wanting to believe everything will be fine,
but I stay behind.
Shrewdness and realization fill up the
empty space;
I've grown fond of this silhouette.
A tendency towards imploding—
I play to disintegrate.

Slow Burn Ballad

In a hasty attempt to circumvent the
crooked deck,
she is one inch away from falling.
It appears her resources are threadbare,
but she does what she can to manage.

Her mere existence is a story
that entails affliction and martyrdom,
and you can tell from the look in her eyes
she wishes she could be elsewhere.
God knows this child is a slow-burn ballad,
trying her best to adhere to an effervescent
orchestra.

Her hands are made of pumice and basalt,
igneous and guileless.
She renders this forlorn dungeon her abode,
and she will continue to do so
until she realizes it is only a childish flight
of fancy
to believe Hephaestus will appraise her
efforts
and finally let her go.

I think I might have said this one thousand
eight hundred times before,
but the more it slips from my lips,
the further the truth goes.
As much as a wisp of heat causes her to
glow,
she is a vaporous force
that magnifies the volcano about to erupt.

Big, Scary World

I want, with all my might,
to see my exertion become something more
than aimless palaver.
Living without doing what I desire
is merely existing—
wantonly, vexed with such charade.

A pragmatic approach to abhorrence,
shuffling blindly towards cowardice.
My dreams are embellished with golden
embroidery;
they catapult me back to the swamp
and negate my caliber.
I step it up a notch,
but my legs are muddled in mire.

Tragedy transpires when the steep
plummeting applauds.
My fears are queuing up;
the thought of feeling anything still terrifies
me,
pervading the air I breathe.
In this bleak and moored boat we call
habitual,
I am stranded without hope.

Propelled on prodrome by oars and
symptoms,
I'm lost in navigation.

You should know I'm just a girl,
trying to make it in this big, scary world.

My Mother's Tongue

My mother's tongue is refined poetry,
an exquisite collaboration between poise
and rhythm.
It is a guardsman dressed in hallelujah—
a symphonic intricacy,
honorific parlance that enlivens the spirit,
drags the soul along with the *erre*,
and makes an eloquent statement.

My mother's tongue is never wrong;
it utters the hardest truths without a stutter,
and I'm thankful a part of me can be
unrelentingly resounding.
My mother's tongue is a precise melody
that filters the deceitful,
never condescending and always so certain,
carrying the indented in each of us like a
pendant—
a string of beads damped in history and
commemoration.

My mother's tongue is my battle cry
and my birthright, even in its absence.
I conflate with certitude this
all-so-grand pride residing within me
and liquidate the rest.

Domination

Where are you safe when the ground
shakes?
In your mother's arms, perhaps?
With your father's hammer underneath
your bunk bed?

When the sun sets indefinitely,
you'll pound every nail in place,
refurbish these pillars which you like to
climb
only to stare off into the distance,
counting the mocking jays passing by.
You are in control, at least for now.

A cunning string wafting through the
scenes,
you reenact the occurrence without
skipping a beat—
with no trepidation in your countenance,
you interfere, impugn the ground that spits
you out.

When you feel the foundation rattling
under the soles of your feet,
the unexpected roar of a territorial beast
who knows no boundaries,
please remember this:
We all long for power, some more than
others.
We take drastic measures to savor the
potency of domination,
and this contrived land has had enough.

To: Marcellus

Reader,

Please don't perish into oblivion;
don't join the graves in their stargazing
wake.
I am telling you not to turn to ashes, only to
be swept away.
Don't become fertilizer for the trees,
pollen for the bees, or anything in between.
The universe has no need for your energy,
but your presence.

Don't cross your eyes and drop your
tongue;
don't ossify your conviction, for you are
not a lamb marching towards the
slaughterhouse.
And if the big, bad wolf is out to get you,
break formation—
sharpen your knife and aim for the jugular.
Procure nothing but courage.

Wake up ruminating on your existence,
and pluck out the barricade with your hard-
boiled claws.

Let the adamant disobedience in you bellow
and budge.
Never forget, Marcellus,
how marvelous it is to be alive.

World of Graft

When I'm feeling high as a kite,
I like to axe the cord, rip off the yoke,
remind myself that I could plunge to the
deepest depths in an instant—
and this tinsel-like armor would strain the
unspeakable in me.

It'd be quite chaotic then,
when I realize I'm not a parrot flying in El
Morro.
I'd sprung out of a marinade of dwelling
sadness,
speaking in salted syllables.

Somehow, my elbows are knee-deep
sunken in gravel,
and I feel all sorts of things except warmth.
One would think I'd be lightheaded after
soaring for weeks,
but this has etched into my scalp quite
easily.

I don't know where I stand in this seafaring
adventure,
jolting out of control each passing instant.
Joy is an unwieldy vessel to nudge.

Feeling volumized comes in different
variations,
with auspicious conditions,
and I briefly reassess the entire situation.

I still say this with grandiose excitement:
Bon voyage, consciousness!
I can't help but slide under the tracks
in this colossal world of graft.

Fickle and Frail

These palm trees stand so tall,
tilting their heads up with zest—
they pledge to touch the starry skies.
In this prohibited landslide,
they are weary of considerations
and well acquainted with the night.

I witness their endeavoring hands
prance around this astral array,
and I wonder how they manage
to survive the rains of May.
I suddenly feel the weight
of all these lives orbiting around me,
but like most of them,
I rest assured that the sun and the moon
will soon reconcile.

Perhaps we are just foreshadowing
the unerring outcome,
that some things don't last forever,
no matter how much we'd like them to.
So, here I lie, vindicating the undeniable.
We learn this life is too much of a tedious
avenue,
expanding at the slightest change in
weather.

Thus, we willingly take the nearest shortcut,
where the clouds above our nobs
remind us we are fickle and frail.

I Wish You Well

For a day I don't see your face,
you are a cocoon in a mangrove kingdom,
caressed by a buckeye butterfly.
Held forth and kind—main stage, front line.

I wish you well, today and all the days to
come.
I say these things like I swallowed my
tongue,
and now it's steady in the back of my
throat,
locked away, I'm sure,
for there's no need to expose my flaws.
My pride halfway goes, and we both know
what this means.

I'm not equable, my liege, and I will never
be.
This lieu, direly and tirelessly apprehensive
at account of fleet, and I fear not,
for it is time to loosen my grip.

Tale of Woe

The first year feels like running backwards,
and there's a sense of unfamiliarity
that justifies the cold, sunken sensation
that here the grasslands lack saturation.

Here, the waves are intimidatingly
ferocious—
which reminds me, once again,
I should've learned how to swim.
Maybe it's taking me longer than I
anticipated
to get used to the climatic changes.

The second year approaches, quick and
impatient,
and I'm still figuring out how to set up my
alarm
because I don't want to wake up before the
sun does.

Non compos mentis—
the third year rears its ugly head,
ready to put the last nail in our coffin.
I digress—
this place has a distinct aftertaste.

Like a lineage of tragedies,
it's a tale of woe.
One can stand idly by
and watch this place go down in flames,
and it still wouldn't feel like home.

Bona Fide Sorcery

Her laugh is the mimicry of a saint's weep,
escapades of matutinal mischief—
an outflow of foreign currency,
unclean and unsteady.

Her legs are heavy, but her arms are
lightweight;
she sets the siege, and you fall for the bait.
They say she's bad news, mate—
a syndicate of bona fide sorcery,
a mix of uniformity and subtle misfit.

What an inconvenience,
how she manages to sweep you off your
feet so easily.
A missile rocket in your pocket,
ready to take off any moment,
but it lingers on until your eyes bulge out of
their sockets.

You count in sheep,
because that's the only way to fall asleep.
She haunts your dreams,
and you believe it is just the beginning.

She says she's not made of stone
or steel—
that she's allowed to feel,
smitten with deckled sunshine,
escaping tyranny and the scarcity of
rainfall,
borne the weight of a yoke of bliss instead.

She's a trammel you thought you'd
overcome,
a ghost you can't kill but have shaken off.

Loose Pendulums

Sometimes lies reign,
prowling voraciously until all we can
hear—
a repertory inferno unraveling in our ears,
strewn over our memories, eager to adhere.

Fibs are always told with concordance,
the kind that mangles the innocent
and those roughed up around the edges,
a scaffolding sustaining our weakened
spirits.

Like loose pendulums without equilibrium,
we swing freely but hang undone.
Dates are just frothed numbers in a rolling
gale,
swirling seething moments we have only
planned out.

But time has its repercussions,
and gabbing on does not mean letting go.
A name can be stained,
but a heart cannot be daubed or besmirched,
a sheaf of ostentation attached
to the same navel as whatever you want
to vouch as legitimate.

A moment of unbridled dismay—
lies levitate and propagate like viruses,
but it's better to be perceived as
pusillanimous
than to feel like our world is collapsing.

Home of the Giants

I am floating over a timeframe
established by your primacy,
concealing the crannies you've plastered
with cement.
I swallow the fairness my buds will never
curry;
I am famished in the eyes of the world.

Dallying with a tincture of desire,
thawing the norms molded by fanatics.
In the home of the giants,
I am a woman whose vision is an act of
defiance,
a lesser being tattooed with sin.

Dressed in flesh, my skin is a dowelled
maze,
adjourned until you can rephrase.
Pure as a desirous getaway;
a senile whimper, a pummeling hum,
perpetuating your sobriety,
inhaling the blaze from your vintage lungs.

My autonomy isn't up for debate,
but you insist it must be political to behave
humanly.

The acclivity of my skeleton,
a quiet resource—more impeccable
than any flattery you buzz my way;
bigger than the disputes you adjudicate.

We don't speak the same dialect;
my knees will never bend to your
cannonball waves,
for I can handle the pressure—
so, I'll have it my way.

Empathy

There is a perilous line between living for
others and living for yourself.
The butterfly effect of either is perpetually
misconstrued.
Sometimes, I'm bewildered by the
unreachable unison in the middle—
the nestle in which the world of iniquity
swells instead of receding.
The small hitch of variety woven into
disconnection, where humanity molders
and empathy warbles away.
Love is not present to object,
so, hate intercedes,
bringing misery to earth,
and somehow people still vote in favor.

Life of the Party

Agnes is the ghost of a friend who never
made it home,
the life of the party, except we're all
dressed in black.
She is sheer sentiment, a hazy laughter
that only brings tears to your eyes—
the memory of a brief rush of bliss
that sailed too quickly.

She is the thought of *what could've been*
that keeps me up at night,
the tangled expression that clothes my
façade
when they ask me about jumble cookies.

The gentle simmering rage inside me
tells me I must keep moving,
but my feet are glued to the tile.

She is the song of my past that whispers in
my ear,
I am part of you, too.

Wilderness

My eyes speak of the unknown,
of which my soul has yet to get a slice of.
My hands are the root of my dreams;
they build an empire in the thick of
nothingness.
My body is the wilderness you can only
imagine.

I am a storm that lacks no element,
but space to unwind.
I like messes, but I don't like to be the
cause of them.
I often find myself picking up the pieces of
broken paintings
after the pigment bonds with the plaster—
fresco and pastel on oil canvas,
an opus inspired by kindliness.

My legs are the hunger of an elephant,
a rebellion that can't be tamed until it's fed.
They desire to walk and run,
to discover new horizons,
and jump into the danger zone.

There's nothing more inconceivable than
me—
my heart brims with different colors,
and turmoil is its form of art.

High Spirits

I built a home for myself in the depths of
the ocean,
where sharks cruise through the hallways
and smile inordinately.
The doors are made of theatrical seaweed,
and the ceiling looks like a whale's belly.

Here, the tides are quite subtle,
except for the mermaid's spurt and
occasional meddling.
Dolphins deliver letters through holes in the
walls;
the starfish in the compartment envelopes
them all
and sends them to my friends all around the
globe,
making the ground shake and the kitchen
palpitate like no other.

This little house smells of high spirits.
If you come inside, where it looks
sufficiently wide,
you'd sense it right away.
Though I wouldn't have much to say,
for we don't get many visitors.

At night, it looks slightly haunted,
but we could set up some lights if you
wanted,
make the moon look less like herself
without feeling taunted.

I'd do this just for you,
but you can tell your mother too, to tag
along.
I'd set up the teapot and sing you both a
song,
one that makes you love me,
one that makes you feel enamored.

Female Lead Drama Club

Sometimes, when you leaned in to kiss me,
I was already thinking ahead—
slip your hand up my dress.
Other days, I frankly did not feel a thing.

My cord of thoughts formed curved
passages,
while yours idled vaguely, more stationary,
stirring around one single idea:
that every time you were down for it,
I must be laid out for it,
perched at your disposal like a forensic
mannequin.

My body: an auditorium with no assembly,
and somehow, you still perceive it as a
threat.

I dig my nails into my wrist,
drive them deep to quell the sting,
to suppress my discontent,
otherwise known as cinematic fuss—
female lead drama club.

What else would it be known for?

Maybe Someday

We were reaching for the stars,
but caught ourselves relying on the edges of
our own concept of love—
the type of connection that glistens and
spawns like dots in the sand,
or a flock of gulls by the seashore.
We caught feelings for each other like mice
in the night,
and waded deeper within our delusion.
I held your heart in the palm of my hand
until it started to ebb away on my
fingertips,
and your keen-like-a-blade touch sheared
through my chest.
Now I look back and see how our footsteps
intermingled,
tearing down unattainable flags
and crushing milestones along the way,
forming a single path to *maybe someday*.

Peak of Pry

There once was a side of curiosity
where my distrust now resides—
a peak of pry deluding me,
tantalizing my judgment.

I am suddenly fobbed by their ploys,
employed in written form.
Some seeds rely on birds for dispersion,
but like minute droplets,
my words are soluble on your tongue.

Your translation and my reality
go on a moonlight tryst,
where your guile is the chief obstacle
that makes my truth totter and fall.

Twelfth Grade

Supposedly, teenage mentality
is the ruckus I accommodate
in my day-to-day.
Stacking blocks that quickly collapse
when I practice introspection.

My psychologist suggests
I build up my concentration.
My motto, "Independence and autonomy,"
grants me little regulation.

Jumping through hoops,
my mental gymnastics
hinder my cognitive development—
identity formation, depression.
Swift decline and faulty ethics—

This is the bruising that never fades,
onto the twelfth grade.

Willow Dove

I am but a mere appendage of the man,
tippy-toeing around hot coals—
pejorative connotations,
serving from dusk till dawn.

I am a willow dove bearing catkins;
conciliatory cooing in the morning,
flapping my pliant branches in the evening,
yielding osiers for basketry.

What a pity, such a frowzy feeling—
to be used to giving and never receiving.
The willow dove must advocate for peace,
even if the pigeon's serenity
comes at the expense of her own.

Contemplate the reactionary attitudes like
the reflection in a mirror;
trace the outline of your beak,
recognize the wood
from which you were carved.

You are real,
but not entirely conceivable.

Baby, there is no turning page.
Yes, the aches will intensify—
there is no need to be dense
and continue to denigrate yourself.

Be the tree;
spread your roots,
steady your nerves.

Grace Rodriguez is a Puerto Rican writer and poet residing in New Jersey, USA. She works as an interpreter and aspires to share her passion for poetry and fantasy through her writing.

www.ingramcontent.com/pod-product-compliance
Lightning Source LLC
Chambersburg PA
CBHW060032050426
42448CB00012B/2964